T0343852

The Three Pigs

A Fairy Tale • Retold by Lee Petrokis

These are the three pigs. They are brothers. Their names are Pedro, Paco, and Pablo. They live next to each other.

Pedro lives in a straw house. Pedro is sitting in his armchair. He looks out his window.

The big, hungry wolf is in front of Pedro's house!

The wolf blows down Pedro's house!

Run, Pedro! Run!

Pedro runs out the door. He runs to Paco's house.

Paco lives in a stick house. Paco and Pedro are behind the sofa. The wolf is in front of Paco's house!

6

The wolf blows down Paco's house!

Run, Paco! Run, Pedro!

They run out the door. They run to Pablo's house.

Pablo lives in a brick house.

"The wolf can't get in here," says Pablo.

Oh no! The wolf is above the pigs!

8

"I can't blow down this house," says the wolf. "But I can climb into it!"

Facts About Houses

People live in different kinds of houses all around the world. Look at these houses from different countries.

Thailand

Argentina

Japan

Russia

How are all these houses the same? How are they different?

Mongolia

Greece

Fun with Houses

Write the word.

behind	in front of	above	next to

The 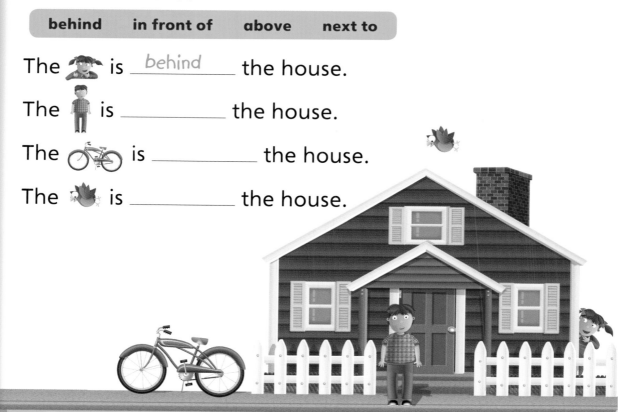 is _behind_ the house.

The is _____ the house.

The is _____ the house.

The is _____ the house.

14

Color the picture.

window 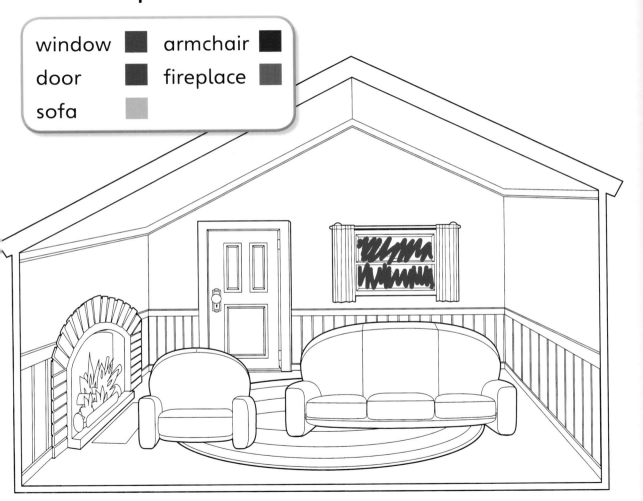 armchair
door fireplace
sofa

Glossary

blows

brick

fire

same

stick

straw